C000143633

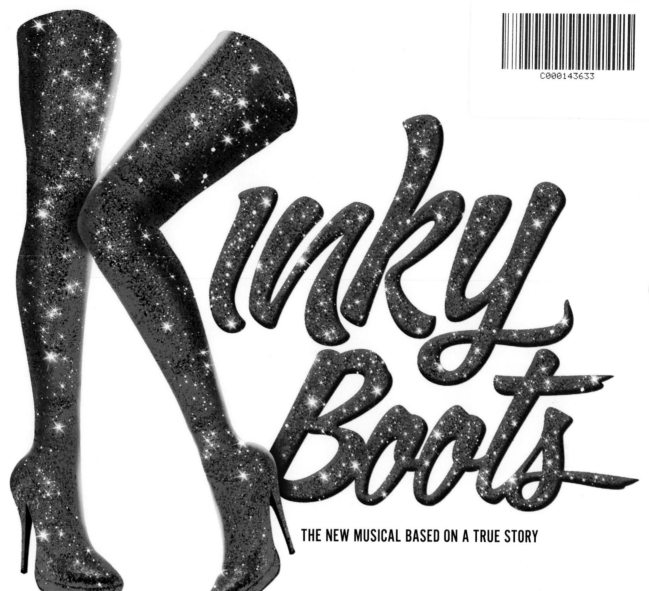

THE NEW MUSICAL BASED ON A TRUE STORY

BOOK BY
HARVEY FIERSTEIN

MUSIC AND LYRICS BY
CYNDI LAUPER

DIRECTED AND CHOREOGRAPHED BY
JERRY MITCHELL

BASED ON THE MIRAMAX MOTION PICTURE *KINKY BOOTS* WRITTEN BY **GEOFF DEANE & TIM FIRTH**

Produced by
Alfred Music Publishing Co., Inc.
P.O. Box 10003
Van Nuys, CA 91410-0003
alfred.com

Printed in USA.

ISBN-10: 0-7390-9836-5
ISBN-13: 978-0-7390-9836-3

Special thanks to MARK FRIED at Spirit Music Group for giving Alfred Music the opportunity to produce this songbook.
We appreciate the loyalty and friendship you have shared with us for all these years. —The Team

Stark Sands

Stark Sands, Billy Porter, and Angels

TOP LEFT: Billy Porter and Stark Sands; Annaleigh Ashford; **TOP CENTER:** Stark Sands, Annaleigh Ashford, and Billy Porter; **TOP RIGHT:** Full Company;
TOM LEFT: Billy Porter; **BOTTOM CENTER:** Stark Sands, Annaleigh Ashford, Stephen Berger, Andy Kelso, and Billy Porter; **BOTTOM RIGHT:** Billy Porter

DARYL ROTH   HAL LUFTIG

JAMES L. NEDERLANDER   TERRY ALLEN KRAMER   INDEPENDENT PRESENTERS NETWORK
CJ E&M   JAYNE BARON SHERMAN   JUST FOR LAUGHS THEATRICALS/JUDITH ANN ABRAMS
YASUHIRO KAWANA   JANE BERGÈRE   ALLAN S. GORDON & ADAM S. GORDON
KEN DAVENPORT   HUNTER ARNOLD   LUCY & PHIL SUAREZ   BRYAN BANTRY
RON FIERSTEIN & DORSEY REGAL   JIM KIERSTEAD/GREGORY RAE
BB GROUP/CHRISTINA PAPAGJIKA   MICHAEL DeSANTIS/PATRICK BAUGH
BRIAN SMITH/TOM & CONNIE WALSH   WARREN TREPP   AND JUJAMCYN THEATERS

present

Book by
HARVEY FIERSTEIN

Music & Lyrics by
CYNDI LAUPER

Based on the Miramax motion picture Kinky Boots
Written by Geoff Deane and Tim Firth

starring

STARK SANDS   **BILLY PORTER**

ANNALEIGH ASHFORD   CELINA CARVAJAL

DANIEL STEWART SHERMAN   MARCUS NEVILLE

PAUL CANAAN   KEVIN SMITH KIRKWOOD   KYLE TAYLOR PARKER   KYLE POST   CHARLIE SUTTON   JOEY TARANTO
ANDY KELSO   TORY ROSS   JENNIFER PERRY   SEBASTIAN HEDGES THOMAS   MARQUISE NEAL
ADINAH ALEXANDER   ERIC ANDERSON   EUGENE BARRY-HILL   STEPHEN BERGER   CAROLINE BOWMAN   COLE BULLOCK
SANDRA DeNISE   JONAH HALPERIN   ERIC LEVITON   ELLYN MARIE MARSH   JOHN JEFFREY MARTIN   NATHAN PECK
ROBERT PENDILLA   LUCIA SPINA   TIMOTHY WARE

Scenic Design	*Costume Design*	*Lighting Design*	*Sound Design*
DAVID ROCKWELL	**GREGG BARNES**	**KENNETH POSNER**	**JOHN SHIVERS**

Hair Design	*Make-up Design*	*Associate Choreographer*	*Casting*
JOSH MARQUETTE	**RANDY HOUSTON MERCER**	**RUSTY MOWERY**	**TELSEY + COMPANY**
			JUSTIN HUFF, CSA

Music Director	*Music Coordinator*	*Technical Supervisor*	*Production Stage Manager*
BRIAN USIFER	**MICHAEL KELLER**	**CHRISTOPHER C. SMITH**	**LOIS L. GRIFFING**

Associate Producer	*Advertising*	*Marketing*	*Press Representative*	*General Management*
AMUSE INC.	**SPOTCO**	**TYPE A MARKETING**	**O&M CO.**	**FORESIGHT THEATRICAL**
				AARON LUSTBADER

Music Supervision, Arrangements & Orchestrations by
STEPHEN OREMUS

Directed and Choreographed by
JERRY MITCHELL

CONTENTS

PRICE AND SON THEME

Words and Music by
CYNTHIA LAUPER
Arrangement by
STEPHEN OREMUS

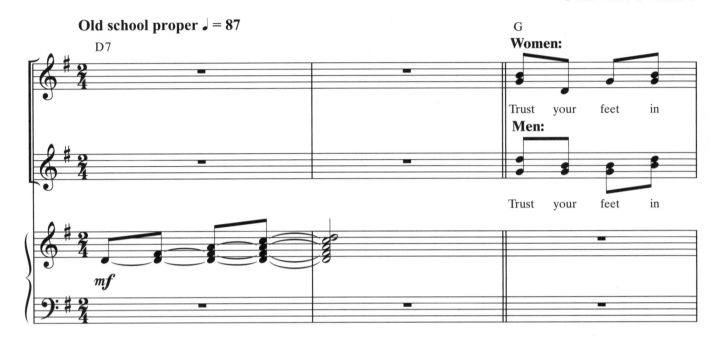

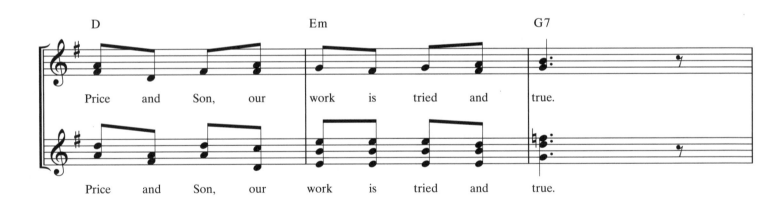

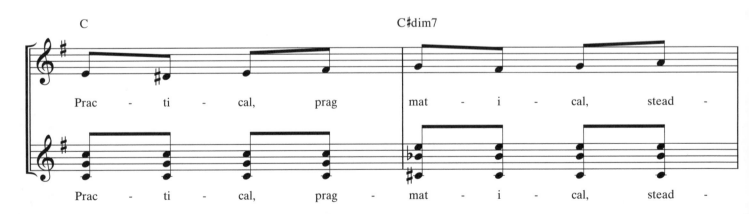

Price and Son Theme - 2 - 1

Seque to "The Most Beautiful Thing"

THE MOST BEAUTIFUL THING IN THE WORLD

Words and Music by
CYNTHIA LAUPER
Arrangement by
STEPHEN OREMUS

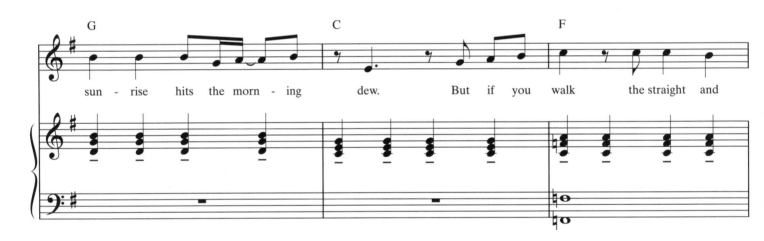

Mr Price: *Do you know what the most beautiful thing in the world is, Charlie?*
Young Charlie: *A shoe.*

The Most Beautiful Thing in the World - 17 - 1

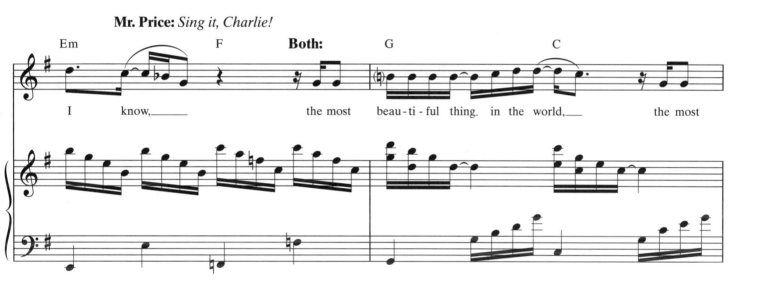

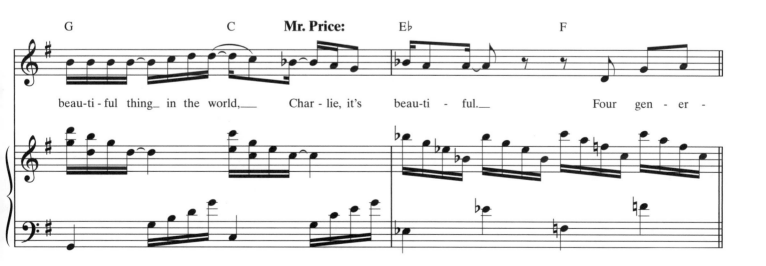

Mr. Price:

a - tions__ have paved the way__ be - fore__ you. You'll be next in line__ when my time is

All Women:

Ha, ha, ha, ha.__ Ooh.__ Ha, ha, ha, ha.

Male workers:

Ha, ha, ha, ha.__ Ooh.__ Ha, ha, ha, ha.

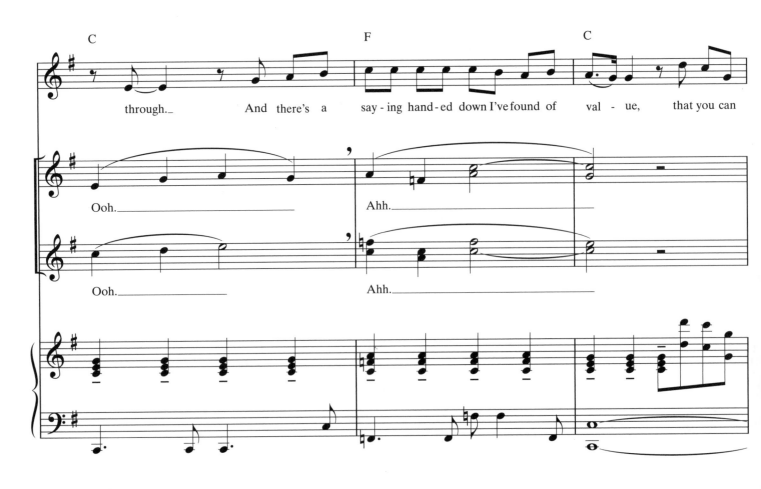

through.__ And there's a say - ing hand - ed down I've found of val - ue, that you can

Ooh.__ Ahh.__

Ooh.__ Ahh.__

Young Charlie: *But what if I don't want to make shoes?*
Mr. Price: *You're a right funny kid, you are.* [GO ON]

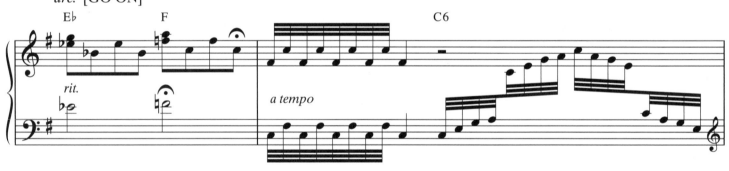

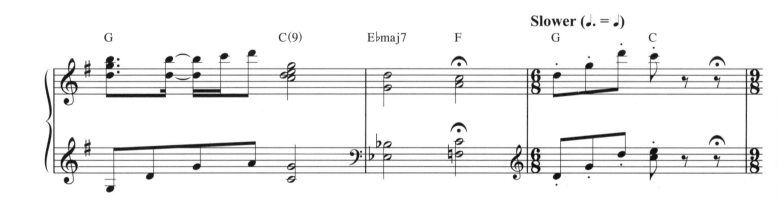

Simon Sr.: *Take those things off your feet and get inside here! Stupid boy!* [GO ON]

Nicola: *Charlie, here are the shoes I told you about. Come have a look-see.*

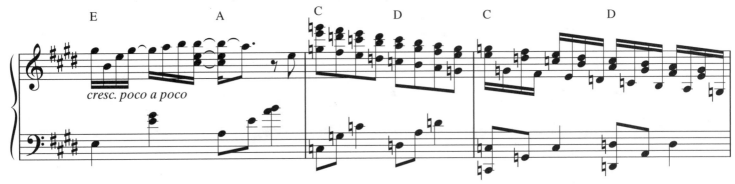

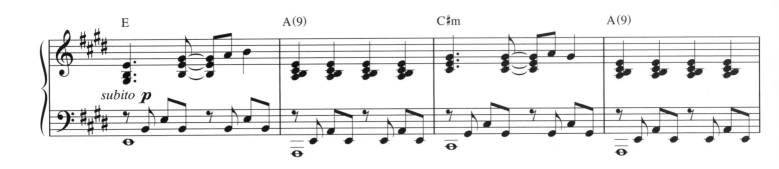

Nicola: *Aren't they the most necessary things ever? If you want to slip a ring on my finger, you'll first slip these shoes on my feet.*
Charlie: *It's a tad posh for life in Northampton, wouldn't you say?*

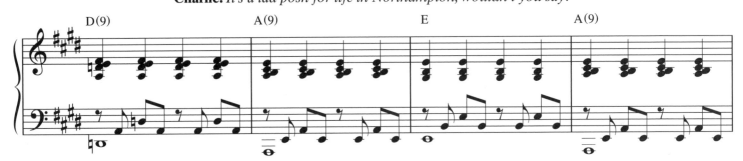

Nicola: *Then good thing we're moving to London. And won't they make a fitting farewell to the stink of cattle farms and tanning leather? We may have been born in a small factory town, but we sure as hell don't have to die there.*
Charlie: *You see the price? There's three month's rent.*
Nicola: *Pinch 'em or pay for 'em, That is up to you. But these shoes are in my future.*

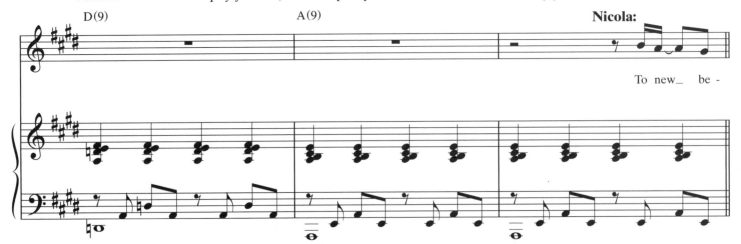

To new_ be -

Mr. Price: *Your life, your future is right here at this factory. You belong here.*
Charlie: *No, Dad, I belong with Nicola in London.*
Mr. Price: *No, you belong here.*
Charlie: *Will you toast my journey?*

Mr. Price: *But, to leave your home and family for a job shopping in London...*
Charlie: *Marketing, Dad. Richard Bailey has offered Nicola and I positions marketing real estate.*
Mr. Price: *You're breaking my heart, Charlie.*

24

Charlie: *To you, Dad.*
Mr. Price: *Shoes can protect a man's journey, but only his heart can choose the path.*
And so a toast to our own Charlie. May you never fail to point your shoes back home.

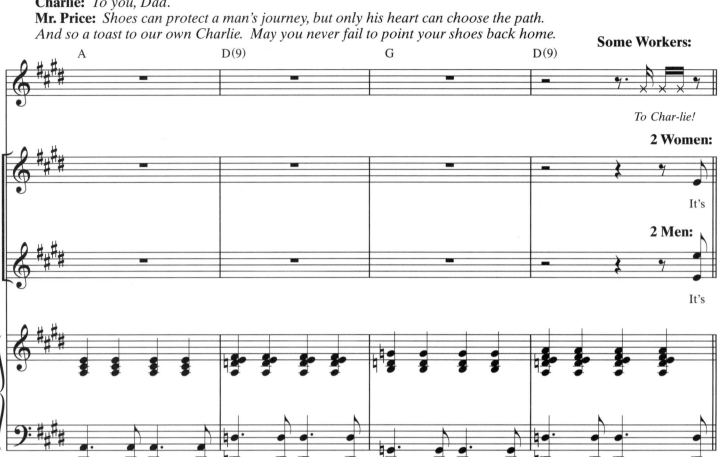

TAKE WHAT YOU GOT

Words and Music by
CYNTHIA LAUPER
Arrangement by
STEPHEN OREMUS

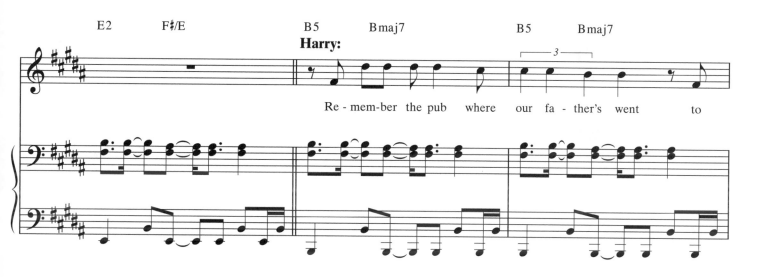

Take What You Got - 8 - 1

Heavier

with the times_ move to Lon - don - town or live out a leg - a - cy.

Well, may - be this time I take a chance

leap in - to the vast ex - panse._ May-be this time I_

_ seize my_ des - ti - ny, my des - ti -

Harry: If you're on the wrong road - turn back.
Charlie: So, you'll help me out? Thank you, Harry.

Harry:
Two! Three! You've got - ta take what you got.

Harry+ Company (lower harmony):
Ev - en when your life is in

Company:
Take what you got.

knots. You take aim, take your shot. Some -

Take your shot.

LAND OF LOLA

Words and Music by
CYNTHIA LAUPER
Arrangement by
STEPHEN OREMUS

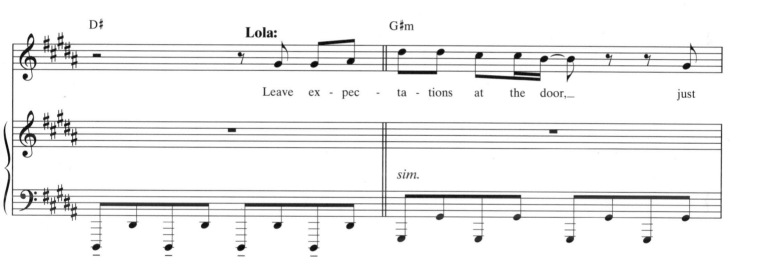

40

Land of Lola - 10 - 4

Lola: *No need to be embarrassed. I like being looked at. And you like to look. I know a way to make us both happy.*

46

CHARLIE'S SOLILOQUY

Words and Music by
CYNTHIA LAUPER
Arrangement by
STEPHEN OREMUS

Mellow rock ♩ = 110

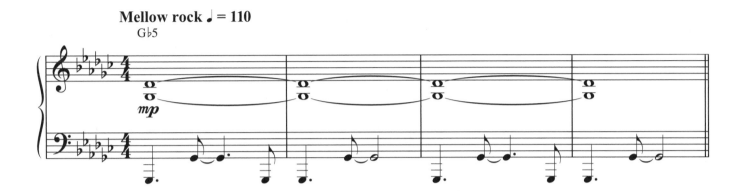

Charlie:

Do I be-long here? Am I what's wrong here? Know what I'm do-ing? Or

am I a fraud? Do I fit in? Where do I be-gin?

Charlie's Soliloquy - 3 - 1

STEP ONE

Words and Music by
CYNTHIA LAUPER
Arrangement by
STEPHEN OREMUS

Rock ♩ = 138

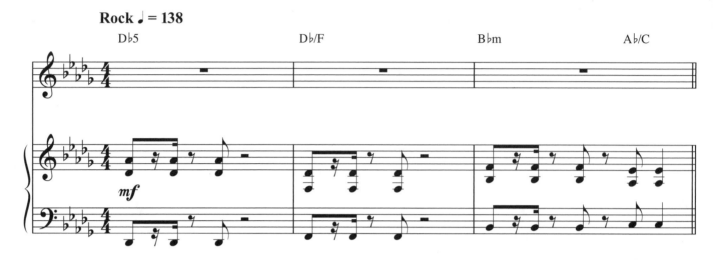

Verse 1:

1. This is time for a shake__ up, look at me wake__ up__ tak-ing con-trol.__

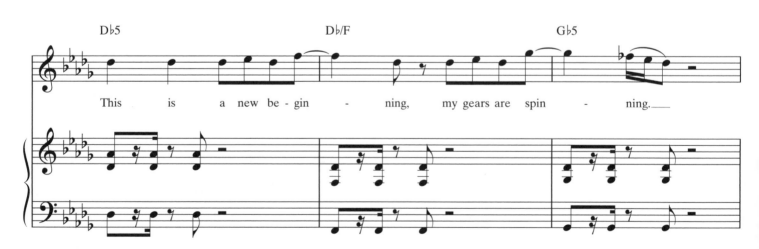

This is a new be-gin - ning, my gears are spin - ning.__

Step One - 7 - 1

SEX IS IN THE HEEL

Words and Music by
CYNTHIA LAUPER
Arrangement by
STEPHEN OREMUS

Sex Is in the Heel - 15 - 1

Am

sert - ing   ac - tual   sci - en - tif - ic   rea - son   heels   tense   the   leg   and   the   hind - quar - ter   re - gion,

Lola: *That's the scientific view.*
But you know what I say?

lift - ing   the   rear   and   mak - ing   it   ap - pear   pert   and   read - y   for   mat - ing   sea - son.

Lola:

The   sex   is   in____   the   heel____   fierce   as   you   can____

make   it.____   The

sex is the__ ap - peal.__ Kin-ky Boys can shake it.__

Pump it up 'til it's os - ten - ta - tious. Funk it up it's con - ta -

Women:

Pump it up! Funk it up!

Angels:

Pump it up! Funk it up!

Lola:

gious.__ The sex is in__ the heel__ so just em - brace-

Lola:
From Lon - don to Mi - lan,_____ stil -

Women:
From Lon - don to Mi - lan,_____ stil -

Angels and Men:
From Lon - don to Mi - lan,_____ stil -

Sex Is in the Heel - 15 - 9

68

Lauren: *These are brilliant. I'd wear any one of them.*
Charlie: *You're not our niche market.*
George: *These are some very interesting ideas here.*
Charlie: *They're all stiletto heels. It's physically impossible to make a stiletto that can bear the weight of a full grown man."*
George: *Not so fast.*

George:

If we could

Slow Russian boom-chick

mold the steel,   one piece from ball to heel,   we'd un-der-pin it, and re-make it so not

Charlie: *Sorry?"*
George: *I said... [GO ON]*

Charlie: *Yeah? You think?*
George: *We can do it.*
Lauren: *We can do it.*
Charlie: *We can do it! [GO ON]*

THE HISTORY OF WRONG GUYS

Words and Music by
CYNTHIA LAUPER
Arrangement by
STEPHEN OREMUS

Verse 1:

makes you in - se - cure, makes you so un - sure, is so im - ma - ture, loves his moth - er more,

colla voce
N.C.

or... has a girl - friend named Ni - col - a. Er...

a tempo
drums

Chorus:
B♭5   F   C5

Char - lie,_____ hon - est - ly,___

F   B♭5   F

_____ I've been hurt___ like this___ be -

NOT MY FATHER'S SON

Words and Music by
CYNTHIA LAUPER
Arrangement by
STEPHEN OREMUS

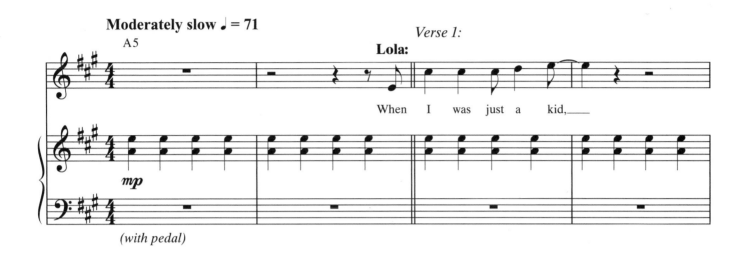

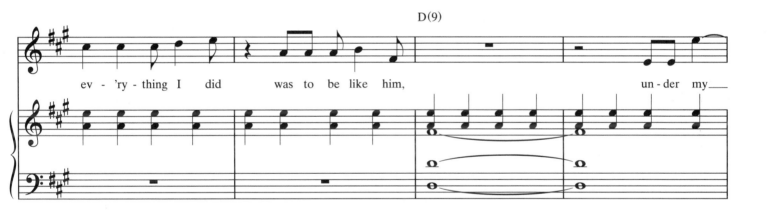

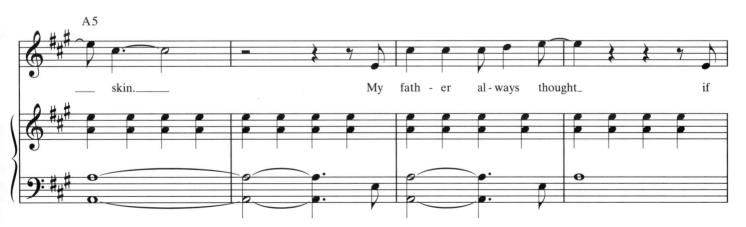

Not My Father's Son - 9 - 1

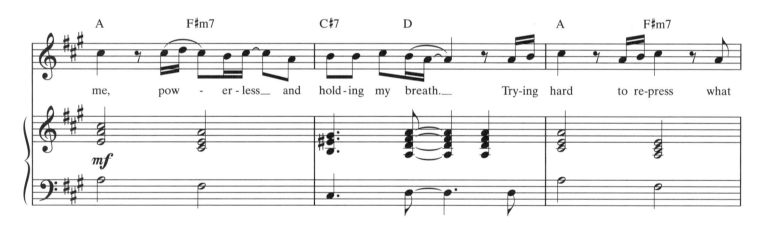

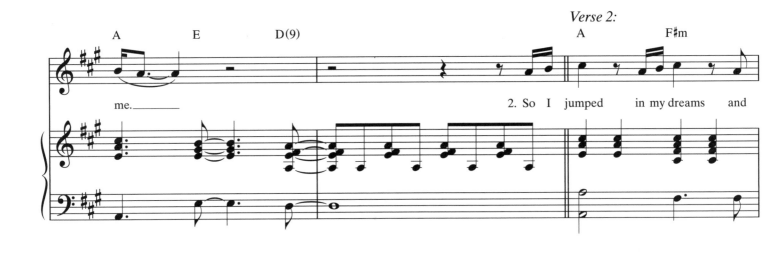

Bridge:

The end - less tor - rent of ex - pec - ta - tions____ swirl - ing in - side my____ mind.____ wore____ me down.____ I came____ to the rea - li - za - tion and I fin - 'lly turned a - round____ to____ see_____ that I____

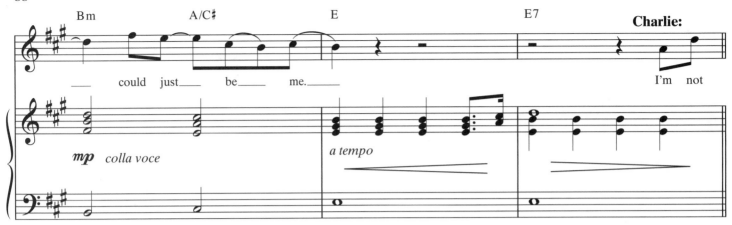

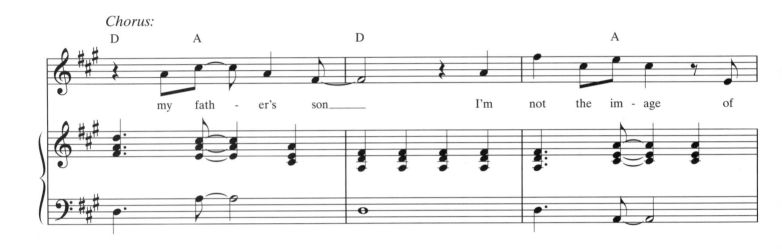

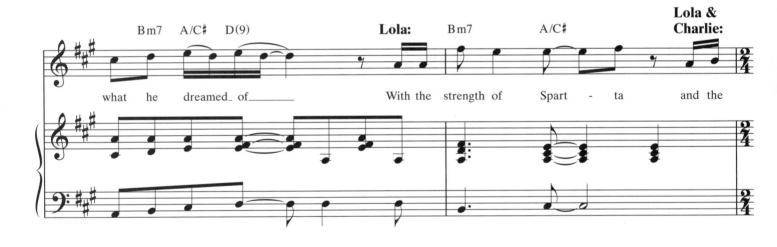

to ech - o what he'd done_____ and mir - ror

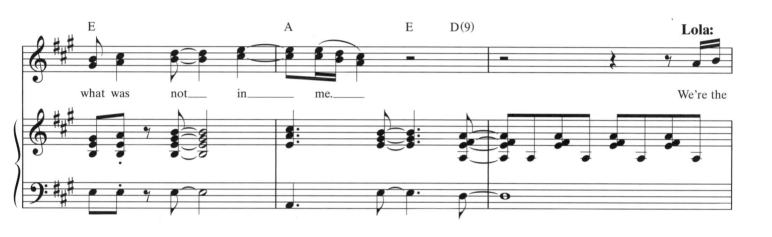

what was not___ in___ me.___ We're the

Slightly slower

same, Char - lie boy, you and me.___

Lola: *Charlie from Northampton, meet Simon from Clacton.*
Charlie: *Let's make boots!*

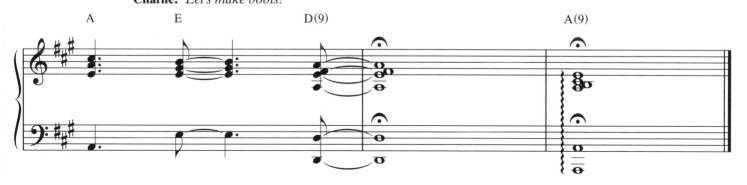

Not My Father's Son - 9 - 9

EVERYBODY SAY YEAH

Words and Music by
CYNTHIA LAUPER
Arrangement by
STEPHEN OREMUS

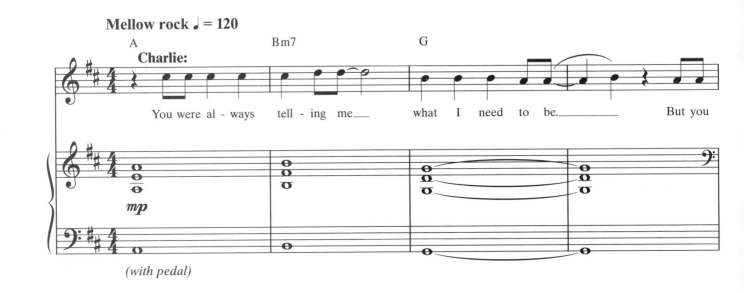

Charlie: You were al-ways tell-ing me__ what I need to be.__ But you

nev-er real-ly had e-nough faith in me.__ Dad, you gave up the fac-to-ry.__ Well,

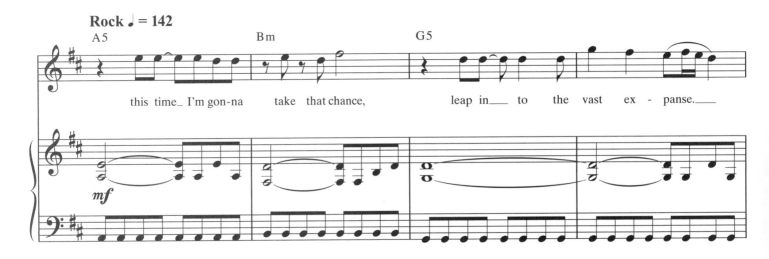

this time__ I'm gon-na take that chance, leap in__ to the vast ex-panse.__

94

Charlie: *Welcome to our future. No longer are we making shoes.*
We are making two and a half feet of irresistible tubular sex. So let's do it!

Male Worker: **2 Female Workers:** **Pat:**

I punched the holes. I sewed___ the seams. And I pull__ the leath - er tight._____

George: **All Women:** **Charlie:**

I put the steel in - side_____ the heel. Now we go off like dy - na - mite_____ Can you

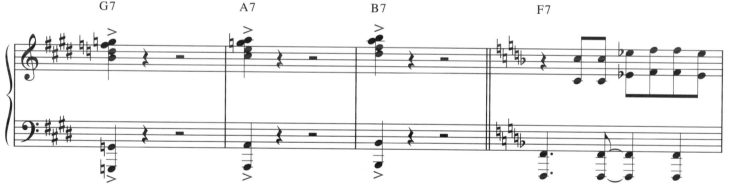

100

Everybody Say Yeah - 14 - 11

WHAT A WOMAN WANTS

Words and Music by
CYNTHIA LAUPER
Arrangement by
STEPHEN OREMUS

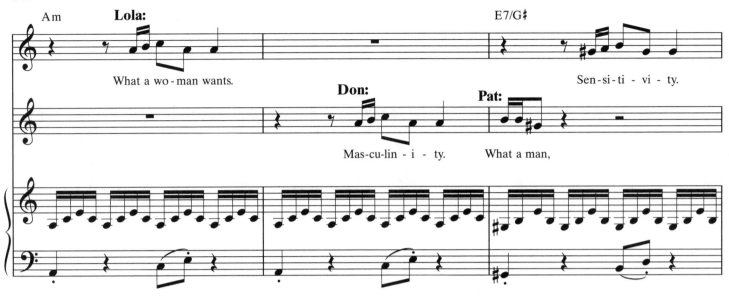

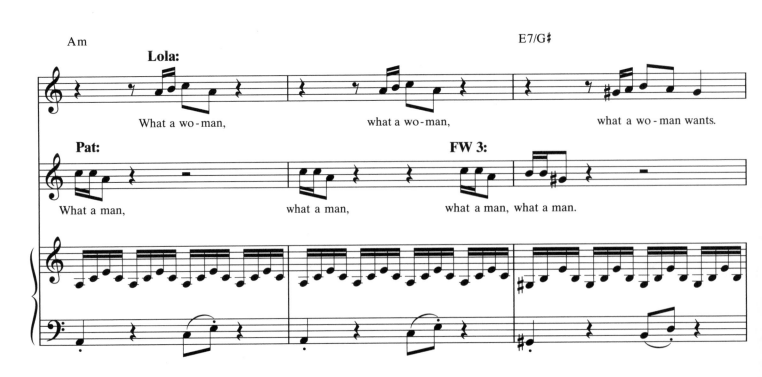

Don: *Come on, we all know that what a bird really wants is a rock solid...*

110

112

Don: *Piss off.*
Lola: *I have a challenge for you: Write down what you think I need to do to be a real man. I'll do the same for you. Whatever you tell me to do, I will have to do. BUT, you will have to do the same for me. Deal?*

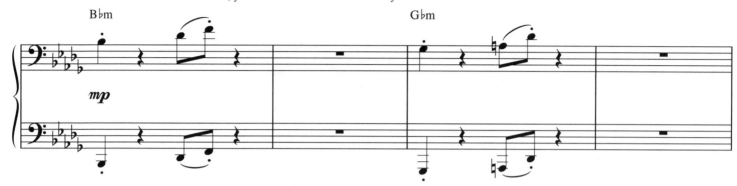

Don: *I ain't wearin' no poufy dress.*
Lola: *Chickening out already? [GO ON]*

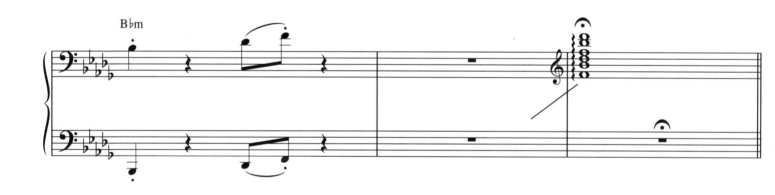

What a man,   what a man,   what a man. What a man,   what a man,   what a man.

IN THIS CORNER

Words and Music by
CYNTHIA LAUPER
Arrangement by
STEPHEN OREMUS

Driving Rock ♩ = 97

MW 3: *Um hmmm. Looks like there's gonna be trouble.*

Angel 3: *Oo-wee. He don't know who he's messin' with. Uh. Huh.*

Angel 2: *Ladies, Gentlemen, and those who have yet to make up your minds...*

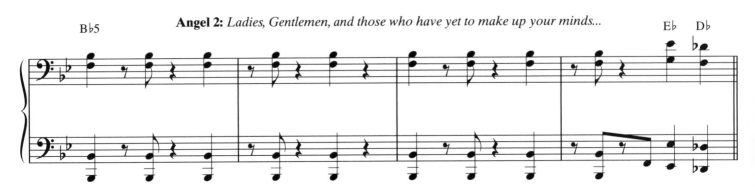

Trish: *Who do you think you are? Coming to our town lookin' like a penny sardine on a five-star plate.*

You better watch your back.

Trish/MW 3:

Don's Team:

Hit him off his high heels. Hit him in the

cheek and send him back to Lon - don town.

Trish:
Se - quined freak.

Pat: *You're just gonna get slapped, slapped, slapped.*
Angel 2: *Listen up, you two. I want a clean, fair, but artfully performed fight. I don't want to see any blows below the belt or any hairs out of place. Hang on, darling, you've a tick of lipstick on your teeth. All right then. Get to your corners... [GO ON]*

Angel 2: *(cont.) ...and come out fighting!*

Trish: *He ain't half the man Don is!*
Pat: *You can say that again!*

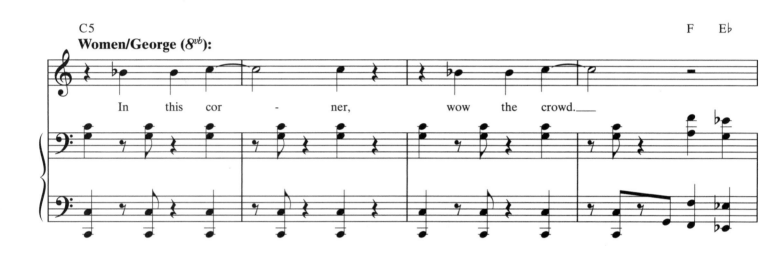

Angel 2: *Back to your corners, you beasts!*
Angel 3: *Care for a Grasshopper, darling? It'll keep ya bouncy.*
Pat: *If you finish him off fast we can still get Kimchee at the Korean's.*

Half-time feel

up - per - cut, a left hook, and a pir - ou - ette too!

(drums)

8vb

Referee Angel:

Db   D

Round   two!

Eb   **All except Don & Lola:**   Ab   Eb   Ab

Hit him in his big mouth.   Hit him in his in - se - cu - ri -

Hit him in his big mouth.   Hit him in his in - se - cu - ri -

a tempo

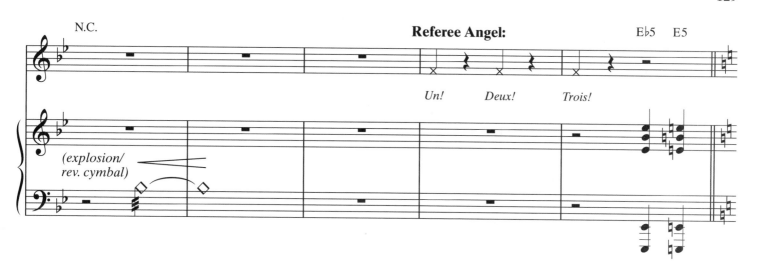

In This Corner - 15 - 14

CHARLIE'S SOLILOQUY
(Reprise)

Words and Music by
CYNTHIA LAUPER
Arrangement by
STEPHEN OREMUS

Charlie:
Who was I kid-ding this scheme was skid-ding, my frac-tured at-tempt_ at

tak-ing con-trol.___ I tried in___ vain,___ now I'm to blame.___

Charles Soliloquy - 2 - 1

Now I'm___ left___ with___ a deep dark hole. So con - fi - dent,

so col - lect - ed and___ so cool._____ Hey,

look at___ me now...___ *I'm a fool.*

SOUL OF A MAN

Words and Music by
CYNTHIA LAUPER
Arrangement by
STEPHEN OREMUS

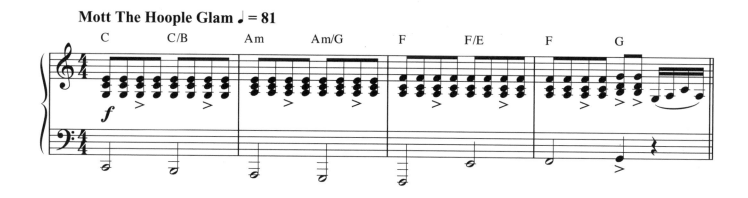

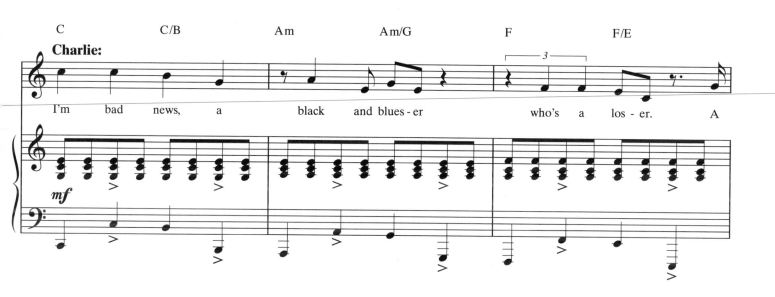

Soul of a Man - 7 - 1

Just when I'm reach-ing for__ that rung at the top, I'm that bro-ken heel_ un-stead-y and

read-y read-y to drop._ When will I be the soul of a man__
Soul of a man._

no - ble and wise____ like the soul of a man_ who lift-ed me high__
Ooh____ Soul of a man._ High._

HOLD ME IN YOUR HEART

Words and Music by
CYNTHIA LAUPER
Arrangement by
STEPHEN OREMUS

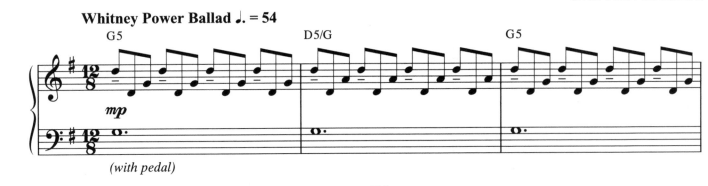

Hold Me in Your Heart - 5 - 1

is stand-ing in front of you_____ and loves you___ a-ny-

way._____ Hold___ me in your heart till

you un-der-stand._____ Hold___ me in your heart just

___ the way that I am._____ With all your faults I love you, don't

RAISE YOU UP / JUST BE

Words and Music by
CYNTHIA LAUPER
Arrangement by
STEPHEN OREMUS

Dance Club tempo ♩ = 122

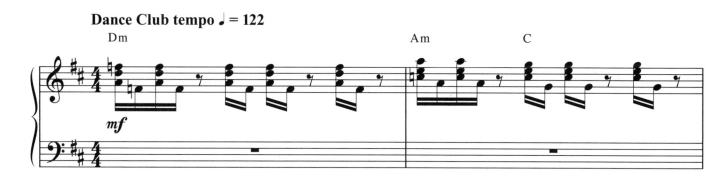

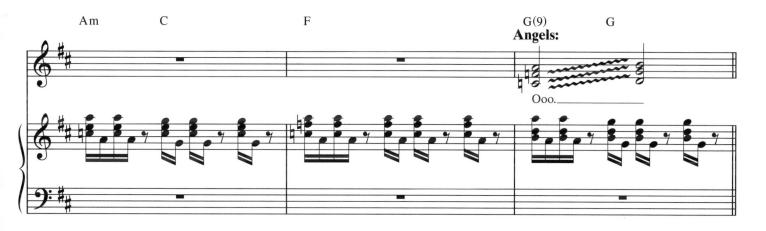

Angels:
Ooo._____

Lola:
Once I was a-fraid__ but then you came a-long, you put your faith in me and I was

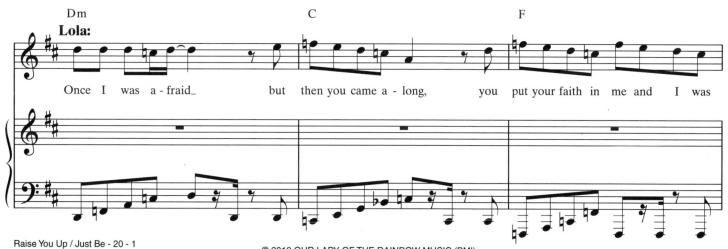

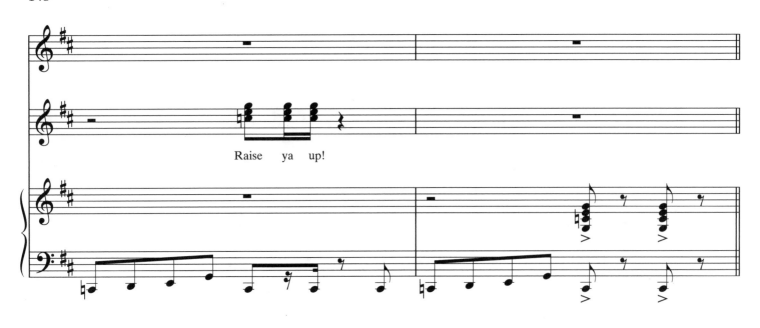

Raise ya up!

Dm   C   F

Charlie:

Ne-ver put__ much heart   in an-y-thing be-fore.   You strut in-to my life and help me

G   Dm   C

go for some-thing more.   Now I stand up for my-self.   Now I stand out from the crowd.

Angels:

Ooh._____

152

Lauren: *Wait! Wait! Wait! Wait! Hold it right there buster. Are you saying you'd like to take me out?*
Charlie: *Yes.*
Lauren: *Are you saying that you and Nicola are through?*
Charlie: *Yes.*
Lauren: *Are you saying that you are actually available?*
Charlie: *Yes.*
Lauren: *And you still like girls?*
Charlie: *Yes.*
Lauren: *Carry on!*

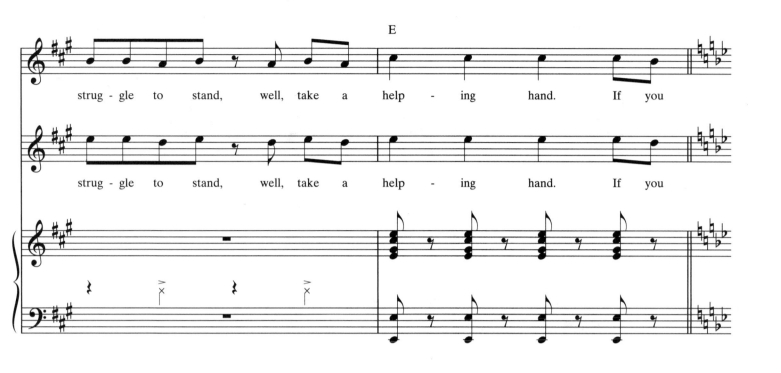

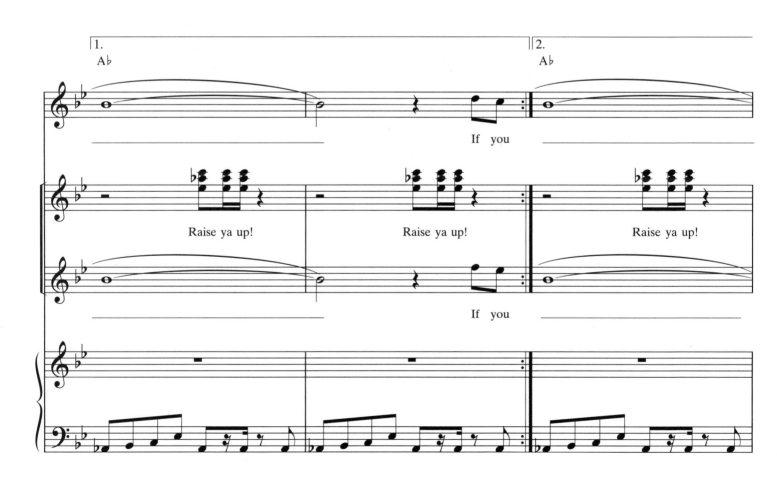

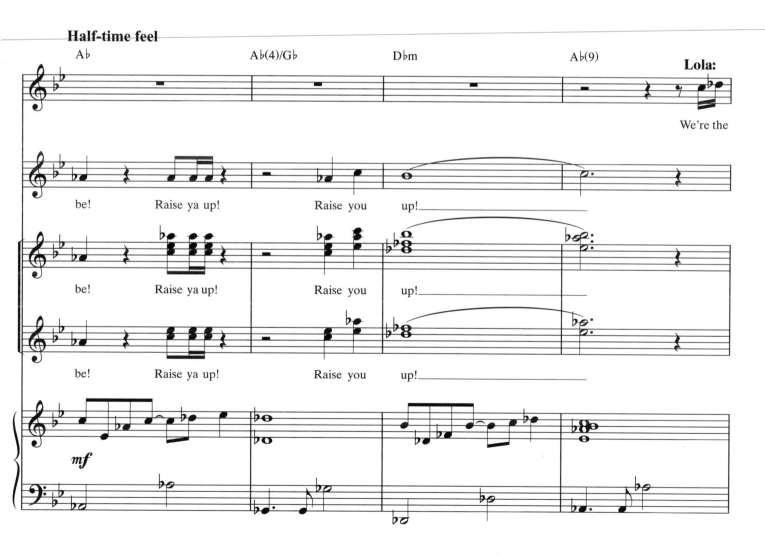

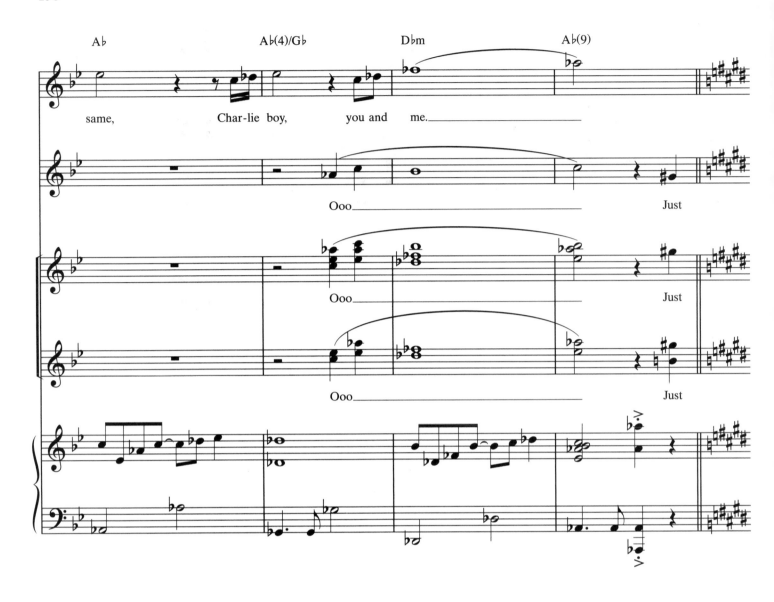

Groove!

Lola: *Ladies...*
Charlie: *Gentlemen...*
Both: *...and those who have yet to make up their minds.*

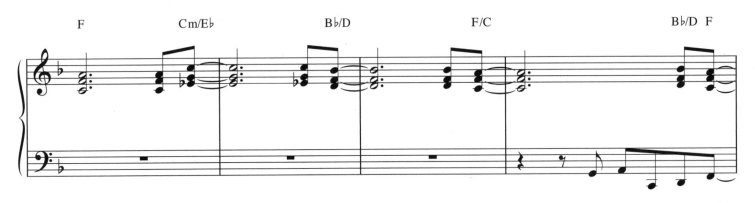

Charlie: *As people all over the world clamor for Kinky Boots... it is time for us to get back to work. But before we go, we'd like to leave you with the 'Price & Simon secret to success.*
Lola: *Alright, now we've all heard of the Twelve Step program have we not, yes? Well, what you can do in twelve, I want you to know that we all can do in six.*

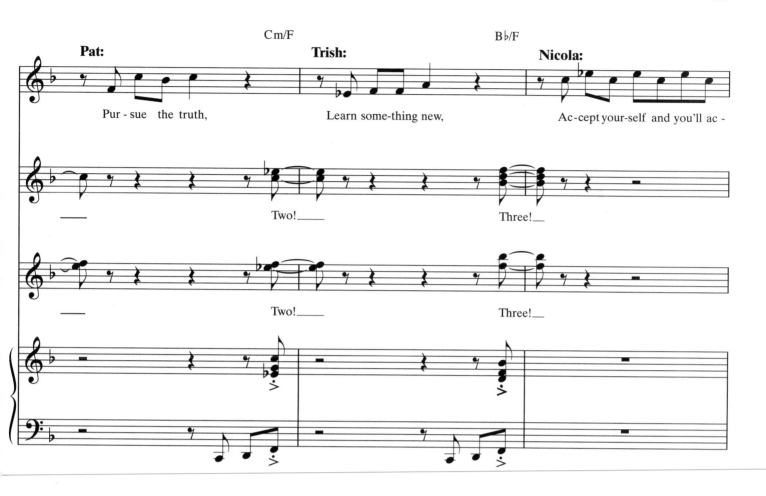

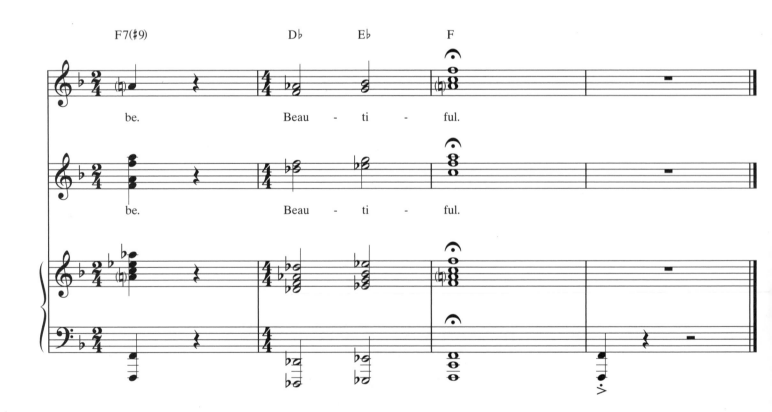